LIFE'S LIKE THAT

OR POEMS FOR WRINKLIES

BY

JOYCE BURTON

A Bright Pen Book
An Authors OnLine imprint

ISBN10: 0-7552-1068-9
ISBN13: 978-0-755210-68-8

Authors OnLine Ltd
19 The Cinques
Gamlingay, Sandy
Bedfordshire SG19 3NU
England

This book is also available in e-book format, details of which are available at
www.authorsonline.co.uk

Bright Pen

Introduction

Joyce Burton is a poet who uses her own experiences in Life to inspire her poetry. This collection is mainly aimed at the more mature reader, but both young and old will hear echoes of their own lives in many of the poems.

Joyce is married, a mother, four times a grandmother and a dog-lover. She has always delighted in the Cumbrian fells and although she no longer does the "big climbs" she and her husband still enjoy being out in the Lakes, not far from their Cockermouth home.

CONTENTS

Illustrations

From original oil paintings by Eileen Clark

Fifty years on

We climbed the fellside in the pouring rain
In the first few months of our love.
No anoraks then, no waterproof trousers, no boots
To protect from the storm from above
An oiled cycle cape and sou'wester
Walking shoes with nails and tricounis
We were soaked straight away
And our feet squelched all day
Through the bogs and the streams on the fellside
At last we stood by the tarn
And we kissed
With our faces streaming wet.
And the love and the joy and the passion –
I remember yet.

Five minutes more

I sit on the pebbles on the river shore
Watching the water and the mayflies.
The sun is setting but I'll have five minutes more.
That's the trouble with us mortals
We always want five minutes more.
Of youth, of love, of life, of laughter.
We've never had enough.

The wind blows cold and I shiver.
Why can't we say, 'that day was good'
And like the mayfly fold our wings
And gently slip away down river.

Children

When you are young
And money's short
Your house is shabby
And cold and dark
But children fill the house with laughter
Sadly it's only after
They've spread their wings
And gone
And your house is clean
And bright and smart
That you realise
That it's lost
It's heart.

Forgiveness

I have a problem with forgiveness.
I don't think you can make yourself forgive
It comes unbidden
Like love
Its roots are hidden
And if you do forgive
Can you forget?
Have you forgiven?
You see
I have a problem with forgiveness.

The Sun

He was lying
In the bottom
Of a box of odds and ends
At a car boot sale.
A big yellow sun
With a great big smile
Abandoned in a pile
Of this and that
A splash of creosote
Marred his forehead
"You can have him for twenty pence"
The stallholder said.

I took him home
Cleaned him up
Painted him bright yellow
And fixed him to the fence
He was part of a water feature
Cupped hands outstretched
For the water from the fountain
That would never come.

I felt an affinity for him
I have a drawer
Full of things I'll never do.
The embroidered tablecloth
I'll never finish
Knitting patterns I'll never knit
Recipes I'll never cook.
Photographs I never manage
To put into a book

But today it rains
The rain in his cupped hands
Overflows in a waterfall.
He has his day after all
And as I watch with a smile
Time slips quietly through my fingers
And in a little while
Is gone.

The moment of birth

The baby is here at last
Small and wrinkled but perfect
It's a boy
And I lie with him
In a golden bubble of joy
I know it will burst 'neath the pressure
Of washing and feeding and sleepless nights
But now I'm at the end of the rainbow
I can smile, I can laugh, I can sing
And who cares what tomorrow may bring.

The February Moon

Here is the February moon
And here comes the high tide

You can keep your scientific explanation
For the moon and the seas eternal motion

It's a love affair I think
As on the morning
I watch the full moon sink
Into the ocean.

Floating on the Tide

I went down to the shore
To say Goodbye.
Holidays at an end
Sun setting
In the western sky.
Alone, no-one there to see
I kicked off my shoes
Suddenly young and free
And ran to paddle in the sea.
The waves with their ebbs and floes
Pushed the sand between my toes.
I giggled.
I felt only five
And glad to be alive.

Then I saw the buoy
Floating on the tide
Broken free from the side
Of a boat.
I must have it
I went in to my knees
And managed to seize
it and waving it aloft
Splashed back to the beach.

Secretly I packed it in my bags
Crushing my clothes into rags
But now it hangs on my kitchen wall
A reminder for me to see
That the child is still alive and well in me.

My friend – Ben

My friend is black and white
With three red legs
He comes to me and begs
For chocolate
He's a dog of course.
He was a stray
A bag of bones and tattered fur
And getting on in years
His eyes quite blank – no love, no tears
"He's a bother", the lady said.
And so he was.
Leave the door on the jar and out he'd go.
Or forget to shut the garden gate
He'd sidle out, he wouldn't wait.
But slowly he settled in
A big, kind, gentle dog.
He obeys my husband's every word
But he and I are equals - friends
I think he is unique,
For he is a stoic.
And he's taught me
Courage and acceptance of my fate.
And I've taught him the joy of friendship
And the lovely taste of chocolate.

The Sting

I was sitting in the garden
Quietly resting,
When a wasp flew by.
It landed on my wrist
And stung me.
It made me cry.

And life's like that
It stings you for no reason
At any age or any reason.
There's no grand plan
It's all quite random.
And all you can do
To relieve the pain
Is put on the dolly blue
And start again.

Outside my barge window

The world outside my barge window
Is all green
The dark green waters of the river
Slide gently by.
The rushes at the edges stand five feet high.
And every shade of green.
The willows on the banks hang their long branches
down
Covered in light green leaves – dancing, graceful
and trailing
In the dark green water.
And there's a flash of green where the kingfisher
glides
And the glint of a green head from the rushes
Where the mallard hides.
From my barge the world is as it must have been
One hundred years ago
Quiet and soft and green, all green.

The Eclipse

I stood looking up at the moon
High in the sky
Round and full and yellow.

I knew all the reasons
From Science
For what was to follow.
The shadow crept slowly over its face
Covering it bit by bit.
It was still hanging there up in space.
But suddenly it turned dark dark red.

I knew that it would
So tell me why should
I suddenly feel as I did.

Dark forces from out of the long ago
Rushed into my head.
Ancient fears from people long dead.
The universe tilted and turned
As the blood red moon burned
In the sky.
I can't explain why.

The Enemy

He's behind you all your life
Through days of peace and days of strife
Creeping and crawling and slithering there
But you don't care
You're much too busy,
To think of him.
Sometimes as you get older
You glance over your shoulder
And catch a glimpse of him.
But his face is dim
Though you might feel
His breath and know he's real
But as life draws to its end
You must turn and face him
And then you'll find to your surprise
He is your friend.

The Reluctant Cook

My mother-in-law was a wonderful cook
And all in her head, not from a book.
Four cooked meals a day she made
And every one was top grade.

So when I married her only son
I knew lots of cooking had to be done.

First of all soup, not out of a tin of course
But bacon bones boiled for hours and hours
To try to reconstruct her powers
With vegetables carefully peeled and cut -

But-

I forgot the bones bubbling on the stove
And they all boiled dry filling the house with
smoke
Which made my husband choke and choke.

End of soup.

The skin on my rice puddings blackened and
burned
The milk in my sauces went lumpy and turned
My sponge cakes rose and fell in again
My fries were too greasy and gave him a pain.

He bought me a book
On how to cook.
I have it yet
You can see the wet
Marks of my tears
And the pages stained with grease and with flour.
And soon my love began to sour.

So I gave up trying to cook like his mom
And kissed him instead
And took him to bed.

A Modern Fairy Tale

So I'm well past three score and ten
When
I get a letter from the N.H.S.
Do they want to help me with good food?
Or give me something to lift my mood?
Or do I need a little extra care?
Oh No! They want me to wear
Padded knickers!
Do they want to help me to hear the phone?
No they want me to wear padded knickers
Lest I crack a bone.

I tell them that I much regret, but no
I don't want to grow
Fatter still.
Maybe old ladies built like fairies
Will do their best for their research
And wear the knickers as they fly
Landing, safely padded, from on high.

Technology

The vacuum spews out muck
The video's got stuck
The T.V. screen is full of snow
The cooling fan refuses to blow.
The toaster burns the toast.
The microwave gives up the ghost.
Good job I've got no internet
That would print rubbish
You can bet.

So should I go back to using a broom?
On my hands and knees scrubbing a room?
Cooking on an open fire that I have to keep
stoking?
Not a chance in hell! - you must be joking.

The Accident

Dashing down the stairs
In the middle of a row
I slipped and fell – I don't know how
And landed on the floor
Beside the front door
With my ankle twisted round and round.
Luckily an x-ray found
It badly sprained, but still unbroken.
So here I am limping still.

The moral of this tale is clear.

If you want to shout and rant and swear
Make sure you're sitting comfortably
In a large and easy chair.

Woman – Man

Trained to follow
Two steps behind
Head held low
Gentle caring kind
She's a woman

Trained to lead
Getting his own way
Life tailored to his need
In control of the day.
He's a man

In the 21st Century
Are they now hand in hand
Walking to the promised land
Both of them equal
Two heads held high?

Well pigs might fly!

Dead Already

Walking through a lovely wood with my dog
I passed a couple eating lunch, sitting on a log
My dog is blind and could not see them sitting there.
But smelled the food and stopped sniffing at the air.
The man raised his hand and shouted,' get away!'
And the dog moved on, afraid to stay.
I stopped to explain that he was old and blind
And meant no harm.
Expecting them to smile and succumb to his charm.

But no.

'He should be on a lead,' the woman snapped.
'We don't like dogs, they're dirty,' said the man.

How sad.
Not to feel compassion for his age
Or as he stepped out in the dark
Admiration for his courage.

What good the beauty all around that they can see.
They're dead already.

Halloween

As you walk down the street
To play trick or treat
Watch out – you might meet
A witch on a broomstick
And sitting behind her
A big black cat
He's up in the sky
Cats aren't meant to fly
His yellow eyes wide with fear
So as you get near
Grab him off the broom
And take him home.
Stroke his fur
Hear him purr
A witch's cat in the past
A home cat at last.

You could start a society
To set witches' cats free
Every Halloween.

Autumn

The nasturtiums climb up the fence
Red and orange and yellow
The fruit glows on the trees
Crimson and purple and mellow
The Sedum blossoms brilliant pink
With final nectar for the bees to drink.

Chrysanthemums wave their shaggy heads
Red and bronze in garden beds.
And all the leaves on the trees are turning
In the late bright sunshine burning, burning.
All the colours bold and brave
Defying Winter's cold, dark grave.

Shadows

I walked up the lane
The sun was setting
The light beginning to wane
And my shadow ten foot tall
Up the dry stone wall.

I went into the little old church
At the end of the lane
With the setting sun glinting
On the stained glass pane,
Where candles burned
And flickered in the gloom

And everywhere my shadows darted and
danced
Up the aisle and over the pews
And round the crib of baby Jesus.
It was Christmas Eve.
And even those, like me, who had ceased to
believe
Felt the magic.

I turned and left the church
Outside black darkness had fallen.
No sun, no moon, no shadows.
No Magic.

Energy

I was never told
How when I got old
I'd get so slow
Slow as a tortoise or a snail
Like water seeping through a dyke
My energy must fail

I love my family still,
Fit to kill
But not enough to make the tea
Instead I'll sit and write a poem
Just for you and me.

The Sea

I wakened in the early hours
I don't know why.
I couldn't sleep
So in the end I rose
And sat beside the window
Looking out to where the field
Sloped to the steep cliff
With the dark sea beyond.

And then I realised the field was full
Of seagulls by the score.
And as I watched more and more
Flew in from out the night
Till all the field was white.

Like a great convocation
They walked around, not eating
But quietly greeting
One another.
Then as the eastern sky was tinged with dawn
They all arose and silently were gone.
But I sat on
Wondering.

At last I thought they were the souls of sailors
Who had perished in that dark green sea.
And now returned to glimpse their homeland
In the night.
Then, leaving a blessing on the sailors of today
They rose and fell again
Over the sea on their endless flight.

Memento to my grandchildren

Dear grandchildren
I leave behind
An echo of my love.
Not to bind
You in the past
But give you courage for the future.

I leave behind
A hope
That you will be kind
To my memory
And sometimes think
Lovingly of me.

I leave behind
A prayer
That you will find
Happiness and love too
In whatever you decide to do.

Ashes to ashes and Dust to dust

It seems quite good to me
To think of my dust blowing round the world to
eternity.
I'll drop my dust on my children's children like a
benediction.
Carrying a breath of love long gone
It's just a fantasy, I know, but who can tell?
It's better, I think, than visions of heaven and hell.

From my Window

From my window
I can see
A lovely spreading
Chestnut tree
Green and lush all summer
But now
Autumn tips its leaves with yellow
And the conkers ripe and mellow
Begin to fall.

When winter comes
I shall watch
The tracery of branches
Against the darkened sky.

Beautiful tree
I think you're watching me
Sitting here by my window
As time goes by
Goes by
Goes by

Horizon

I went to a funeral
Church of England.
The usual
A hymn or two
A prayer or two
A word or two
Of comfort from the ordinary vicar.
Fiftyish. Baldish. Roundish face
and then he said
"Death is merely the horizon"
For me he was a poet
A seer, a man of dreams
I left the funeral
Hugging his words.

Death is merely the horizon.

Bare Trees

I suppose most people
Like to see the trees
Part of the Spring and Summer scene
covered in blossom
And clothed in green

Not me
I like to see them in the Winter
Stripped bare of leaves
The branches and the twigs
Making intricate patterns
Against the sky

And people are like trees
In the winter of their lives
The ornaments of youth all gone
You can see the bones of them.
The how, the why, the wherefore
Of the lives they've lived.
The reasons for what they did
In the past. Oh Yes
You can see exactly who they are
At the last.

Earth

I love to lie here on the ground
Listening for the sound
Of the world's heart beating
Others may think
That heaven is up in the clear blue sky.
Not I
For me
Heaven is in the warm brown earth
Teeming with life.

I lie close to it
And I am content
That at the end of life
I will return to it
Here.

Printed in the United Kingdom
by Lightning Source UK Ltd.
124623UK00001B/352-399/A